The Truth About the Doctrine of Discovery

Prepared by

Meru El Muad'Dib

The **Doctrine of Discovery** established a spiritual, political, and legal justification for colonization and seizure of land not inhabited by Christians. It has been invoked since Pope Alexander VI issued the Papal Bull "Inter Caetera" in 1493. The Papal decree aimed to justify Christian European explorers' claims on land and waterways they allegedly discovered, and promote Christian domination and superiority, and has been applied in Africa, Asia, Australia, New Zealand, and the Americas.
https://upstanderproject.org/firstlight/doctrine/

Papal Bull – edict of the pope. Google.com

Pope Nicholas V issued the papal bull Dum Diversas on 18 June,1452. It authorized Alfonso V of Portugal to reduce any "Saracens (Muslims, Moors) and pagans and any other unbelievers" to **perpetual slavery**. This facilitated the Portuguese slave trade from West Africa. The same pope wrote the bull Romanus Pontifex on January 5, 1455 to the same Alfonso. As a follow-up to the Dum Diversas, it extended to the Catholic nations of Europe dominion over discovered lands during the Age of Discovery. Along with sanctifying the seizure of non-Christian lands, it **encouraged the enslavement** of native, non-Christian peoples in Africa and the New World. "We weighing all and singular the premises with due meditation, and noting that since we had formerly by other letters of ours granted among other things free and ample faculty to the aforesaid King Alfonso – **to invade**, **search out**, **capture**, **vanquish**, and **subdue** all **Saracens** Moors, Muslims) and pagans whatsoever, and other enemies of Christ wheresoever placed, and the kingdoms, dukedoms, principalities, dominions, possessions, **and all movable and immovable goods** whatsoever **held and possessed** by them and **to reduce their persons to perpetual slavery**, and to apply and appropriate to himself and his successors the kingdoms, dukedoms, counties, principalities, dominions, possessions, and goods, and to **convert them to his** and **their use and profit** – by having secured the said faculty, the said King Alfonso, or, by his authority, the aforesaid infante, justly and lawfully has acquired and possessed, and doth possess, **these islands, lands**, **harbors, and seas**, and they do of right belong and pertain to the said King Alfonso and his successors". In 1493 Alexander VI issued the bull Inter Caetera stating one Christian nation did not have the right to establish dominion over lands previously dominated by another Christian nation, thus establishing the Law of Nations. Together, the Dum Diversas, the Romanus Pontifex and the Inter Caetera came to serve as the basis and justification for the Doctrine of Discovery, the global slave trade of the 15th and 16th centuries, and the Age of Imperialism. https://doctrineofdiscovery.org/dum-diversas/

(Gilder Lehrman Collection) **The Papal Bull** "Inter Caetera" issued by **Pope** Alexander VI on May 4, 1493, played a central role in the Spanish conquest of the New World. The document supported Spain's strategy to ensure its exclusive right to the lands discovered by Columbus the previous year. Wikipedia

To understand the connection between Christendom's principle of discovery and the laws of the United States, we need to begin by examining a papal document issued forty years before Columbus' historic voyage In **1452**, Pope Nicholas V issued to King Alfonso V of Portugal the bull Romanus Pontifex, declaring war against all non-Christians throughout the world, and specifically sanctioning and promoting the **conquest**, **colonization**, and **exploitation** of **non-Christian nations and their territories**.

According to Marshall, the United States - upon winning its independence in 1776 - became a successor nation to the right of "discovery" and acquired the power of "dominion" from **Great Britain**. [Johnson:587-9] Of course, when Marshall first defined the principle of "discovery," he used language phrased in such a way that it drew attention away from its religious bias, stating that "discovery gave title to the government, by whose subject, or by whose authority, the discovery was made, against all other European governments." [Johnson:573-4] However, when discussing legal precedent to support the court's findings, Marshall specifically cited the **English charter** issued to the explorer John Cabot, in order to document England's "complete recognition" of the Doctrine of Discovery. [Johnson:576] Then, paraphrasing the language of the charter, Marshall noted that Cabot was authorized to take possession of lands, "notwithstanding the **occupancy of the natives**, **who were heathens**, and, at the same time, admitting the prior title of any Christian people who may have made a previous discovery." [Johnson:577] http://ili.nativeweb.org/sdrm_art.html

In other words, the Court affirmed that United States law was based on a fundamental rule of the "Law of Nations" - that it was permissible to virtually ignore the most basic rights of indigenous "heathens," and to claim that the "unoccupied lands" of America rightfully belonged to discovering Christian European nations. Of course, it's important to understand that, as Benjamin Munn Ziegler pointed out in The International Law of when discovered, **were 'occupied by Indians' but 'unoccupied' by Christians**." [Ziegler:46]

Or,

Marshall noted:

On the discovery of this immense continent, the great nations of Europe ...as they were all in pursuit of nearly the same object, it was necessary, in order to avoid conflicting settlements, and consequent war with each other, to establish a principle which all should acknowledge as the law by which the right of acquisition, **which they all asserted, should be regulated as between**

themselves. This principle was that discovery gave title to the government by whose subjects, or by whose authority, it was made, against all other European governments, which title might be consummated by possession. ... The history of America, from its discovery to the present day, proves, we think, the universal recognition of these principles.

Chief Justice Marshall noted the **1455 papal bull Romanus Pontifex** approved Portugal's claims to lands discovered along the coast of West Africa, and the 1493 Inter Caetera had ratified Spain's right to conquer newly found lands, after Christopher Columbus had already begun doing so, but stated: "Spain did not rest her title solely on the grant of the Pope. Her discussions respecting boundary, with France, with Great Britain, and with the United States, all show that she placed it on the rights given by discovery. Portugal sustained her claim to the Brazils by the same title."

On the discovery of this immense continent, the great nations of Europe were eager to appropriate to themselves so much of it as they could respectively acquire. Its vast extent offered an ample field to the ambition and enterprise of all; and the character and religion of its inhabitants afforded an apology for considering them as a people over whom the superior genius of Europe might claim an ascendency. *The potentates of the old world found no difficulty in convincing themselves that they made ample compensation to the inhabitants of the new, by bestowing on them civilization and Christianity, in exchange for unlimited independence.* But, as they were all in pursuit of nearly the same object, it was necessary, in order to avoid conflicting settlements, and consequent war with each other, to establish a principle, which all should acknowledge as the law by which the right of acquisition, which they all asserted, should be regulated as between themselves. This principle

was, that discovery gave title to the government by whose subjects, or by whose authority, it was made, against all other European governments, which title might be consummated by possession.

The ruling maintained that Native Americans — referred to in the decision as "fierce savages" and "the conquered" — **had the right to occupy land, but not full sovereignty**. **It stipulated that tribes were dependent on the federal government.**

If an explorer proclaims to have **discovered the land in the name of a Christian European monarch, plants a flag in its soil, and reports his "discovery" to the European rulers and returns to occupy it, the land is now his, even if someone else was there first**. **Should the original occupants insist on claiming that the land is theirs, the "discoverer" can label the occupants' way of being on the land inadequate according to European standards**. This ideology supported the **dehumanization** of those living on the land and **their dispossession**, **murder**, and **forced assimilation**. **The Doctrine fueled white supremacy** insofar as white European settlers claimed they were instruments of **divine design** and possessed **cultural superiority**.

Ironically, the same year that the *Johnson v. McIntosh* decision was handed down, founding father James Madison wrote: "Religion is not in the purview of human government. Religion is essentially distinct from civil government, and exempt from its cognizance; a connection between them is injurious to both."

Most of us have been brought up to believe that the United States Constitution was designed to keep church and state apart. Unfortunately, with the Johnson decision, the Christian Doctrine of Discovery was not only written into U.S. law but also became the cornerstone of U.S. Indian policy over the next century.
http://ili.nativeweb.org/sdrm_art.html

Using the principle of "discovery" as its premise, the Supreme Court stated in 1831 that the Cherokee Nation (and, by implication, all Indian nations) was not fully sovereign, but "may, perhaps," be deemed a "domestic dependent nation." [Cherokee Nation v. Georgia] The federal government took this to mean that treaties made with Indian nations did not recognize Indian nations as free of U.S. control. According to the U.S. government, Indian nations were "domestic dependent nations" subject to the federal government's absolute legislative authority - known in the law as "plenary power." Thus, the ancient doctrine of Christian discovery and its subjugation of "heathen" Indians were extended by the federal government into **a mythical doctrine** that the U.S. Constitution allows for governmental authority over Indian nations and their lands. [Savage:59-60]

The myth of U.S. "plenary power" over Indians - a power, by the way, that was never intended by the authors of the Constitution [Savage:115-17] - has been used by the United States to:

a. Circumvent the terms of solemn treaties that the U.S. entered into with Indian nations, despite the fact that all such treaties are "supreme Law of the Land, anything in the Constitution notwithstanding."
b. Steal the homelands of Indian peoples living east of the Mississippi River, by removing them from their traditional ancestral homelands through the Indian Removal Act of 1835.
c. Use a congressional statute, known as the General Allotment Act of 1887, to divest Indian people of some 90 million acres of their lands. This act, explained John Collier (Commissioner of Indian Affairs) was "an indirect method - peacefully under the forms of law - of taking away the land that we were determined to take away but did not want to take it openly by breaking the treaties."

d. Steal the sacred Black Hills from the Great Sioux nation in violation of the 1868 Treaty of Fort Laramie which recognized the Sioux Nation's exclusive and absolute possession of their lands.
e. Pay the Secretary of the Interior $26 million for 24 million acres of Western Shoshone lands, because the Western Shoshone people have steadfastly refused to sell the land and refused to accept the money. Although the Western Shoshone Nation's sovereignty and territorial boundaries were clearly recognized by the federal government in the 1863 Ruby Valley Treaty, the government now claims that paying itself on behalf of the Western Shoshone has extinguished the Western Shoshone's title to their lands.

The above cases are just a few examples of how the United States government has used the *Johnson v. McIntosh* and *Cherokee Nation v. Georgia* **decisions to callously disregard the human rights of Native peoples**. Indeed, countless U.S. Indian policies have been based on the underlying, hidden rationale of "Christian discovery" - a rationale which holds that the "**heathen" indigenous peoples of the Americas are "subordinate to the first Christian discoverer**," **or its successor**. [Wheaton:271]

As Thomas Jefferson once observed, when the state uses church doctrine as a coercive tool, the result is "hypocrisy and meanness." Unfortunately, the United States Supreme Court's use of the ancient Christian Doctrine of Discovery - to circumvent the Constitution as a means of taking Indian lands and placing Indian nations under U.S. control - has proven Madison and Jefferson right. http://ili.nativeweb.org/sdrm_art.html

Under various theological and legal doctrines formulated during and after the Crusades, non-Christians were considered enemies of the Catholic faith and, as such, **less than human**. Accordingly, in the bull of 1452, Pope Nicholas directed King Alfonso to "**capture**, **vanquish**, **and subdue the Saracens** (**Moors**, **Muslims**), **pagans,** and other enemies of Christ," to "**put them into perpetual slavery**," and "**to take all their possessions and property**." [Davenport: 20-26] Acting on this papal privilege, Portugal continued to traffic in African slaves, and expanded its royal dominions by making "**discoveries**" along the western coast of Africa, claiming those lands as Portuguese territory.

Thus, when Columbus sailed west across the Sea of Darkness in 1492 - with the express understanding that he was authorized to "**take possession**" of any lands he "**discovered**" that were "**not under the dominion of any Christian rulers**" - he and the Spanish sovereigns of Aragon and Castile were following an already well-established tradition of "discovery" and conquest. [Thacher:96] Indeed, after Columbus returned to Europe, Pope Alexander VI issued a papal document, the bull *Inter Cetera* of May 3, 1493, "granting" to Spain - at the request of Ferdinand and Isabella - the right to conquer the lands which Columbus had already found, as well as any lands which Spain might "discover" in the future.

In the *Inter Cetera* document, Pope Alexander stated his desire that the "discovered" people be "subjugated and brought to the faith itself." [Davenport:61] By this means, said the pope, the "Christian Empire" would be propagated. [Thacher:127] When Portugal protested this concession to Spain, Pope Alexander stipulated in a subsequent bull - issued May 4, 1493 - that Spain must not attempt to establish its dominion over lands which had already "come into the possession of any Christian lords." [Davenport:68] Then, to placate the two rival monarchs, the pope drew a line of demarcation between the two poles, giving Spain rights of conquest and dominion over one side of the globe, and Portugal over the other.

During this quincentennial of Columbus' journey to the Americas, it is important to recognize that the grim acts of genocide and conquest committed by Columbus and his men against the peaceful Native people of the Caribbean **were sanctioned by the abovementioned documents of the Catholic Church**. Indeed, **these papal documents were frequently used by Christian European conquerors in the Americas to justify an incredibly brutal system of colonization** - **which dehumanized the indigenous people by regarding their territories as being "inhabited only by brute animals**." [Story:135-6]

The lesson to be learned is that the papal bulls of 1452 and 1493 are but two clear examples of how the "Christian Powers," or "different States of Christendom," viewed indigenous peoples as "**the lawful spoil** and **prey** of their civilized conquerors." [Wheaton:270-1] In fact, the Christian "Law of Nations" asserted that **Christian nations had a divine right, based on the Bible, to claim absolute title to and ultimate authority over any newly "discovered" Non-Christian inhabitants and their lands**. Over the next several centuries, these beliefs gave rise to the Doctrine of Discovery used by Spain, Portugal, England, France, and Holland - all Christian nations.

"Since we had formerly by other letters (papal bulls) of ours granted among other things free and ample faculty to the aforesaid King Alfonso – **to invade, search out, capture, vanquish and subdue all Saracens (Moors, Muslims) and pagans whatsoever, and other enemies of Christ where so ever placed, and the kingdoms, dukedoms, principalities, dominions, possessions, and all movable and immovable goods whatsoever held and possessed by them and to reduce their persons to perpetual slavery**, and to convert [these properties] to himself and his successors [and these possessions] do of right belong and pertain to the said King Alfonso and his successors." .....Romanus Pontifex

The bull marked the first time the papacy "**made it look as though no one was living there,**" or had any ownership over the land being pursued by European powers, **because there were no Christians there**," Newcomb said. That "**pattern of thought**" then began marching through history. Their idea, or ideas began to march through history. https://oldlife.org/tag/doctrine-of-discovery/

The following is a quote from a timeline of the Christian European Spanish barbarism that was part of the conquering and depopulating of the Americas, provided by Kenneth Humphreys:

"The plunder of the empires of the Americas was to **good purpose**—it allowed Spain to **finance religious persecution** in Europe for over a century. Spanish wars of conquest included laying waste much of the Netherlands and a disastrous attempt to invade England. By destroying diverse cultures in the New World the **Christian conquerors were able not only to eradicate civilizations more ancient than their own but also were able to senselessly erase a vibrant artistic legacy and even scientific knowledge.** In their stead the Christian adventurers imposed a racist tyranny…."

The absolutism of the DOD made its way through the Americas bringing disease to Native tribes and peoples, literally wiping out entire civilizations. In addition, it provided legitimacy for slavery and shipping of Africans to the new world, and the oppression of other ethnic groups. Always it was justified on two major premises; **one**, **bringing Christianity to the savages and heathens of the New World**; and **two, the belief that one race had the divine right and superiority to civilize the world and expand their reach**.

Estimates of the pre-Colombian population of the Americas vary but possibly stood at 100 million—one fifth of humanity in 1492. Between 1500 and 1600 the population of the Americas was halved. In Mexico alone, it has been estimated that the pre-conquest population of around 25 million people was reduced within 80 years to about 1.3 million. In Hawai'i, the population was estimated to be as much as 800,000 at the time of contact in 1798. In less than 60 years, less than 100,000 Native Hawaiians remained.

How could this trail of destruction have been denied for so long? More shockingly, why did post-Columbian America continue the oppression**? The European settlers arrived in "America" to escape the oppression of the old world and the British Empire and then in the 18th and 19th centuries they repeated the exact behavior of their European oppressors**. It was justified under a doctrine called **Manifest Destiny** which upheld the same dogma as the DOD.
https://newsmaven.io/indiancountrytoday/archive/the-sordid-influence-of-the-doctrine-of-discovery-mDI-6yAohUOHrNwv9HJ3RA/

Christopher Columbus Obeys

The first Christian explorer out the gate taking advantage of the papal bulls was Christobal Colon aka Christopher Columbus. He was the first slaver. He was also one of the first to take Americans to the continent of Europe, the Mediterranean, Sicily, Italy, and Africa. Yes, the **opposite way** we are taught in school. We were never taught the slave trade actually started in the Americas and went east initially, then, it traveled the opposite direction. Let us take a closer look.

In any case, b the 1490's Americans were appearing once again in European cities. Pg 21

Moreover, Columbus' impact was singular in that he was, from the first, a dedicated **slaver** and **exploiter** with an extremely callous and indifferent attitude towards culturally different human beings.

Columbus on his first voyage, kidnapped at least 27 **Americans,** two of who escaped, leaving a total of 25 in his hands...Thus, a the very first island reached (Guanani), Columbus already was able to express his willingness to depopulate the entire island in order that the **Americans might be sold as slaves in Europe, or *held as captives in their own land.*** Pg 22

Here, I'd like to point out Martin Luther King's I Have a Dream Speech where he states,

But one hundred years later, the Negro still is not free. One hundred years later, the life of the Negro is still sadly crippled by the manacles of segregation and the chains of discrimination. One hundred years later, the Negro lives on a lonely island of poverty in the midst of a vast ocean of material prosperity. One hundred years later, the **Negro** is still languishing in the corners of American society and **finds himself an exile in his own land**. Martin Luther King 'I Have A Dream'

Several early European explorers and conquistador (exploiters and conquerors), refer to the indigenous people they first met as having copper color or cinnamon colored skin. Some references compare them to Ethiopians and other Africans.

"The **negro** type is seen in the most ancient Mexican sculpture. The **negroes** figure frequently in the most remote traditions of some American pueblos. It is to this race doubtlessly belongs the most ancient skeletons, distinct from the red Americans race, which have been found in various places from Bolivia to Mexico. It is likely that, we repeat, **America was a negro continent**." Carlos Cuervo Marquez

Let us take a look at the 1828 definition of American for more clarity on what is being said without any misunderstanding or anything being misconstrued.

American, *n*, A native of **America**; originally applied to the **aboriginals**, or **copper-colored** races, found here by the Europeans; but now applied to the descendants of Europeans born in **America**. American Webster's 1828 Dictionary

"The American negro of the Great Plains were black and with wooly hair in 1506." Professor Constantine Rafinsque 'The Primitive Black Nations of America'

Not a lot of space will be used to determine the skin color of the aboriginal indigenous people found here by Europeans right now. I believe the point has been made and will be addressed at another time in another book.

His philosophy of **conquest** and **colonialism** was extremely well developed: 'And they are fitted to be ruled and t be set to work, to cultivate the land and to do all else that may be necessary, and you may build towns and teach them to go clothed and to adopt our customs.' Pg 22

After learning of the existence of so-called 'Cannibal' (Carib) groups in the Indies, Columbus began to emphasize the enslavement of the latter. While still at sea, on his first return voyage, Columbus advocated the capture of Caribs: 'very fierce people and well proportioned and of very good understanding, who, **after being removed from their inhumanity**, we believe will be better than any other **slaves** whatsoever.' On January 30, 1494 he addressed to the Spanish monarchs a plan for sending men, women, and children to Spain to learn the Castilian language and to be trained in service,...In other words, Columbus proposed (after his first voyage) that **American slavery** be used to finance the conquest. Pg 22

Thus, even as Columbus was loading five ships with slaves, he was proposing to sell **4,000** in various parts of the **Mediterranean** and along the coast of **Africa**. Pg 23

The shipment of Americans to Europe and Africa by Columbus (and by other Spaniards) was, then, not an accident, nor was it a result of armed resistance or alleged cannibalism. Pg 24

But the tens of millions of Americans who disappeared after 1492 did not all die in the 'holocaust' inflicted within the Americas. **Many thousands were sent to Europe and Africa** where their descendants still live. Pg 25

Now we shall examine data relating to the **Americans** who arrived in **Europe** and along the coast of **West Africa**,...pg 39

All pages are in the book Africans and Native Americans: The Language of Race and the Evolution of Red-Black Peoples by Jack D. Forbes

He captured 1,500 Arawak men, women and children, selected the 500 healthiest among them, and loaded them on his ships.

200 of them died on the **way to Spain**. But Columbus wrote: "Let us in the **name of the Holy Trinity** go on **sending all the slaves that can be sold**."

But he had to find some gold, otherwise his investors would be very unhappy. So, as the historian Howard Zinn writes in his classic A People's History of the United States, "In the province of Cicao on Haiti, where he and his men imagined huge gold fields to exist, they ordered all persons fourteen years or older to collect a certain quantity of gold every three months. When they brought it, they were given copper tokens to hang around their necks. Indians found without a copper token had their hands cut off and bled to death. https://www.livemint.com/Sundayapp/23nihEltoCYOAdHZ0y7JxK/Christopher-Columbus-the-murderer.html

It was at this point in time that his bravery had begun to shift to sheer brutality. His transition is captured in many of the notes that he had sent to the King and Queen of Spain to bolster expectations. In one particular note, he promised: "as much gold as they need and **as many slaves as they ask**."

Soon thereafter he and his men **kidnapped** a number of the Arawaks and forced them to identify other sources of gold throughout the region.

With an extensive arsenal of advanced weaponry/horses, Columbus and his men arrived on the islands that were later named Cuba and Hispaniola (present day Dominican Republic / Haiti). Upon arrival, the sheer magnitude of gold, which was readily available, set into motion a relentless wave of **murder**, **rape**, **pillaging**, and **slavery that would forever alter the course of human history**.

https://www.irishcentral.com/roots/history/truth-columbus-mass-killer-father-slave-trade

Columbus' Own Words

What were Columbus' motivations? What was his personal purpose for sailing to the America's?

The ***Book of Prophecies*** (in Spanish, *El Libro de las Profecías*) is a compilation of apocalyptical religious revelations written by Christopher Columbus towards the end of his life, probably with the assistance of his friend, the Carthusian monk Gaspar Gorricio. It was written between September 1501 and March 1502, with additions until about 1505.

This journal of sorts conveys the medieval notion that in order for the end of the world or the second coming of Jesus Christ to occur, certain events must first be enacted:

1. **Christianity must be spread** throughout the world.

2. **The Garden of Eden must be found** - It was the common belief in the Middle Ages that the biblical Garden of Eden must have been on the top of a crag or mountaintop so that it would not have been affected by the first destruction of the world by flood. Upon arriving in **Venezuela** in 1498, Columbus may have thought that the verdant crags of **Venezuela** bore the garden of the Old Testament of the Bible.

3. A Last Crusade must take back the Holy Land from the Muslims, and that when Christ comes, he will come back in the place he lived and died: Jerusalem.

4. A Last World Emperor must be chosen - Columbus had chosen, at least in his mind, that the Catholic Monarchs, Ferdinand and Isabella, would fulfill this position due to the vast imperial power and religious conviction the Spanish monarchs

claimed. A last world emperor would be necessary to lead the aforementioned crusade against the Muslims and to greet Christ at Jerusalem once the previous steps had been completed. Wikipedia

At a very early age I began to sail upon the ocean. For more than forty years, I have sailed everywhere that people go. I prayed to the most merciful Lord about my heart's great desire, and He gave me the spirit and the intelligence for the task: seafaring, astronomy, geometry, arithmetic, skill in drafting spherical maps and placing correctly the cities, rivers, mountains and ports. I also studied cosmology, history, chronology and philosophy. **It was the Lord who put into my mind (I could feel His hand upon me) the fact that it would be possible to sail from here to the Indies**. All who heard of my project rejected it with laughter, ridiculing me. **There is no questions that the inspiration was from the Holy Spirit**, **because he comforted me with rays of marvelous illumination from the Holy Scriptures, a strong and clear testimony from the 44 books of the Old Testament, from the four Gospels, and from the 23 Epistles of the blessed Apostles, encouraging me continually to press forward; and without ceasing for a moment they now encourage me to make haste**. Our Lord Jesus desired to perform a very obvious miracle in the voyage to the Indies to comfort me and the people of God. I spent seven years in the royal court, discussing the matter with many persons of great reputation and wisdom in all the arts; and in the end they concluded that it was all foolishness, so they gave it up. But since things generally came to pass that were predicted by our Savior Jesus Christ, we should also believe that this **particular prophecy** will come to pass. In support of this, I offer the gospel text, Matthew 24:35, in which Jesus said that all things would pass away, but not His marvelous Word. He also affirmed that it was necessary that all things be fulfilled that were prophesied by Himself and by the prophets. I said that I would state my reasons.

I hold alone to the sacred and Holy Scriptures, and to the interpretations of prophecy given by certain devout persons.
It is possible that those who see this book will accuse me of being unlearned in literature, of being a layman and a sailor. I reply with the words of Matthew 11:25: "Lord, because thou has hid these things from the wise the prudent, and hath revealed them unto babes."
For the execution of the journey to the Indies I did not make use of intelligence, mathematics or maps. **It is simply the fulfillment of what Isaiah had prophesied**. All this is what I desire to write down for you in this book. No one should fear to undertake any task in the name of our Savior, if it is according to His sovereign will even though He gives advice. He lacks nothing that it is in the power of men to give Him. Oh what a gracious Lord, who desires that people should perform for Him those things for which He holds Himself responsible! Day and night moment by moment, everyone should express to Him their most devoted gratitude. I said that some of the prophecies remained yet to be fulfilled. These are great and wonderful things for the earth, and the signs are that the Lord is hastening the end. The fact that the gospel must still be preached to so many lands in such a short time - this is what convinces me.
http://www.christianheritagemins.org/articles/Christopher%20Columbus%27%20Scriptural%20Book%20of%20Prophecies.pdf

Columbus truly felt that he was on a special mission from God. He felt he, was called to sail to the Americas and was serving Jesus. He felt he was the answer to prophecy. This is why, it was no problem, for him to commit the atrocities he did, it, served a bigger purpose. He was spreading Christianity throughout the world. He was fulfilling the great commission. A lot can be said here about him being delusional. Was the slavery, stealing, dehumanizing, rape, and other actions helping to spread Christianity or alienate, separate, and subjugate indigenous people? Or, are these actions religiously sponsored?

Impact of the Doctrine of Discovery

Are the effects of the doctrine still being felt today? How are the indigenous people who are still alive today affected? What is its impact on today's society and culture?

That fifteenth century Christian principle was denounced throughout the session as the "shameful" root of all the **discrimination** and **marginalization** indigenous peoples faced today.

The Permanent Forum noted that, while such doctrines of domination and "conquest", including **terra nullis** and the **Regalian doctrine**, were promoted as authority for land acquisition, they also encouraged despicable assumptions: **that indigenous peoples were "savages", "barbarians", "inferior and uncivilized,"** among other constructs the colonizers used to **subjugate**, **dominate and exploit the lands**, **territories and resources** of native peoples.

According to the text, signs of such doctrines were still evident in indigenous communities, including in the areas of **health**; **psychological** and **social well-being**; **conceptual and behavioral forms of violence against indigenous women**; **youth suicide**; and **the hopelessness that many indigenous peoples experience**, in particular indigenous youth. http://www.un.org/en/development/desa/newsletter/desanews/dialogue/2012/06/3801.html

Terra nullius land that is legally deemed to be unoccupied or uninhabited. In Australia the question of whether British colonizers had regarded the continent as terra nullius at the time of the original settlement, and, if so, whether this was a proper designation, was at the center of several important legal cases in the late 20th and early 21st centuries. wikipedia

The Regalian Doctrine **dictates** that all lands of the public domain belong to the State, that the State is the source of any asserted right to ownership of land and charged with the conservation of such patrimony. Wikipedia

It can be seen within the so-called ‘hoods’ in the ‘inner city’ or ‘ghetto,’ that health, psychological, social well-being, conceptual and behavioral forms of violence against the so-called ‘black’ woman, and a general sense of hopelessness prevails. These things are a direct result of the Doctrine of Discovery.

The ways of life, identities, well-being and very existence of indigenous people are threatened by the continuing effects of colonization and national policies, regulations and laws that attempt to force them to assimilate into the cultures of majoritarian societies. A fundamental historical basis and legal precedent for these policies and laws is the "Doctrine of Discovery", **the idea that Christians enjoy a moral and legal right based solely on their religious identity to invade and seize indigenous lands and to dominate Indigenous Peoples**.

Around the world, **Indigenous Peoples are over-represented in all categories of disadvantage**. In most indigenous communities people **live in poverty without clean water and necessary infrastructure**, **lacking adequate health care**, **education**, **employment and housing**. Many indigenous communities still suffer the effects of **dispossession, forced removals from homelands and families**, **inter-generational trauma and racism**, **the effects of which are manifested in social welfare issues such as alcohol and drug problems**, **violence and social breakdown**. Basic health outcomes dramatize the disparity in well-being between Indigenous Peoples and European descendants.

The patterns of **domination and oppression** that continue to afflict Indigenous Peoples today throughout the world are found in numerous historical documents such as **Papal Bulls**, **Royal**

Charters and court rulings. For example, the church documents **Dum Diversas** (1452) and **Romanus Pontifex** (1455) called for non-Christian peoples to be invaded, captured, vanquished, subdued, reduced to perpetual slavery and to have their possessions and property seized by Christian monarchs. Collectively, these and other concepts form a paradigm or pattern of domination that is still being used against Indigenous Peoples.

Following the above patterns of thought and behaviour, Christopher Columbus was instructed, for example, to "discover and conquer," "subdue" and "acquire" distant lands, and in 1493 Pope Alexander VI called for non-Christian "barbarous nations" to be subjugated and proselytized for the "propagation of the Christian empire." Three years later, **England's King Henry VII followed the pattern of domination by instructing John Cabot and his sons to locate, subdue and take possession of the "islands, countries, regions, of the heathens and infidels** . . . unknown to Christian people." Thereafter, for example, English, Portuguese and Spanish colonization in Australia, the Americas and New Zealand proceeded under the Doctrine of Discovery as Europeans attempted to conquer and convert Indigenous Peoples. In 1513, Spain drafted a legal document that was required to be read to Indigenous Peoples before "just war" could commence. The Requerimiento informed Indigenous Peoples that their lands had been donated to Spain and that they had to submit to the Crown and Christianity or they would be attacked and enslaved.

In 1823, the U.S. Supreme Court used the same pattern and paradigm of domination to claim in the ruling Johnson & Graham's Lessee v. M'Intosh that the United States as the successor to various "potentates" had the "ultimate dominion" or "ultimate title" (right of territorial domination) over all lands within the claimed boundaries of the United States. The Court said that as a result of the documents mentioned above, authorizing "Christian people" to "discover" and possess the lands of "heathens," the Indians

were left with a mere "right of occupancy;" an occupancy that, according to the Court was subject to the "ultimate title" or "absolute title" of the United States. The Johnson case has been cited repeatedly by Australian, Canadian, New Zealand and United States courts, and the Doctrine of Discovery has been held by all these countries to have granted European settler societies plenary power (domination) over Indigenous Peoples, legal title to their lands, and has resulted in diminished sovereign, commercial and international rights for Indigenous Peoples and governments. Europeans believed this was proper based on their ethnocentric, racial and religious attitudes that they and their cultures, religions and governments were superior to non-Christian European peoples.
https://www.oikoumene.org/en/resources/documents/executive-committee/2012-02/statement-on-the-doctrine-of-discovery-and-its-enduring-impact-on-indigenous-peoples

In addition to the subjugation of indigenous peoples, **the Doctrine of Discovery also had a devastating effect on the environment**. **The Discovery Doctrine legally exiled those who had been stewards of their ecosystems for thousands of years and brought in people who had no knowledge of how to care for this land**, **and who based their economy and system on resource extraction**. During the Trail of Tears — the military order of President Andrew Jackson that displaced all Native American Nations in the Southeast to Oklahoma — **extremely valuable knowledge was lost to not only those Europeans in the Southeast about how to care for the land**, but also to the newly settled Native American Nations. As they were trying to adapt to new lands, many of them starved.

The European migrants stripped their new terrain of indigenous forests, **fenced their property lines so their livestock would not wander, and planted what they could**, **often without knowledge of the land**. They simply did all they could to set up a home like they had dreamed about in their home countries. With the support and blessing of laws, and a government in favor of their ownership, the new burgeoning country became a "rich country."

Today, after the rise of the U.S. as a world economic power, many of our global environmental concerns can be traced to this understanding of land ownership and an economic system based on resource extraction. https://www.unitedmethodistwomen.org/news/the-enduring-effects-of-the-doctrine-of-discovery

Further Abuses and Insults to Indigenous People

The **Dawes Rolls** (or Final Rolls of Citizens and Freedmen of the Five Civilized Tribes, or Dawes Commission of Final Rolls) were created by the United States Dawes Commission. The Commission, authorized by United States Congress in 1893, forced the Five Civilized Tribes to agree to a land allotment plan and dissolution of the reservation system.

In order to allot the communal lands, all the citizens of the five tribes (**Cherokee** (**Ketuwah**), **Choctaw** (**Chahta**), **Creek** (**Muskogee**) , **Chickasaw** (**Chikashsha**) , and **Seminole** (**Simanó-li**)) **had to be registered**, including freedmen who had been emancipated after the American Civil War and their descendants. **The rolls were needed as the basis to assign the allotments to heads of household and to provide an equitable division of all monies obtained from sales of surplus lands**. These rolls became known as the *Dawes Rolls*. The Dawes Commission was quickly flooded by applicants from all over the country trying to get on the rolls.

The Commission went to the individual tribes to obtain the membership lists but the first attempts were inadequate. Finally Congress passed the Curtis Act of 1898; it provided that a new roll would be taken and supersede all previous rolls. **Overall the rolls are incomplete and inaccurate for the following reasons**:

many individuals from each tribe were not correctly documented, some individuals were entirely excluded because white census takers didn't believe an individual looked "Indian enough", families had already left Indian Territory after the Civil War, or individuals termed "Blanket Indians" refused to be enrolled because they did not trust the government. These factors created descendants whom are Native American by blood unenrollable in the tribes they descend from. Historian Kent Carter termed people who are Native American by blood, but are unable to enroll because of the previously listed factors the "**Outalucks**".

So some of the indigenous people weren't recorded in the Dawes Rolls because they didn't look 'Indian' enough. How arrogant is it for an immigrant to tell another, on their own land, they don't look the part. (As if the individual telling them that did) There will be some, who, for ridiculous reasons, will not be able to trace their lineage to re-connect with their heritage, lands, languages, and customs. The major reason being, god told foreigners to invade, make perpetual slaves, steal their land, etc. Some were eternally cut off from their past.

In their place, foreigners can now wield political rights, voting rights, healthcare, influence tribal policy and other benefits due to **fraud**.

Tribal citizens were enrolled under several categories:

- Citizen by Blood
  - New Born Citizen by Blood
  - Minor Citizens by Blood
- Citizen by Marriage
- Freedmen (persons formerly enslaved by Native Americans and/or adopted by the Cherokee tribe)
  - New Born Freedmen
  - Minor Freedmen

- Delaware Indians (those adopted by the Cherokee tribe were enrolled as a separate group within the Cherokee)

More than **250,000** people applied for membership, and the Dawes Commission enrolled just over 100,000. **An act of Congress** on April 26, 1906, closed the rolls on March 5, 1907. An additional 312 persons were enrolled under an act approved August 1, 1914. Wikipedia

These so-called **five-dollar Indians paid government agents under the table in order to reap the benefits that came with having Indian blood. Mainly white men with an appetite for land, five-dollar Indians paid to register on the Dawes Rolls, earning fraudulent enrollment in tribes along with benefits inherited by generations to come.**

They were able to steal indigenous peoples' lands and everything that went along with being born (aboriginal) on the continent of North America. Thus obeying the papal bulls that sent them in the first place. It's important to point out that, whether they knew it or not, they were, **through their religious beliefs**, accomplishing the popes goals.

"**These were opportunistic white men who wanted access to land or food rations**," said Gregory Smithers, associate professor of history at Virginia Commonwealth University. "These were people who were more than happy to exploit the Dawes Commission—**and government agents, for $5, were willing to turn a blind eye to the graft and corruption**."

This is why many descendants of Europeans today in America claim to be of indigenous ancestry. Of course they don't know it, but it is a fact nonetheless. Because someone in their ancestry lied, (paid $5), they can legally lay claim to an ancestry they technically don't belong to. How confusing is that?

The **Dawes Commission**, established in 1893 to enforce the General Allotment Act of 1887 (or the Dawes Act), was charged with **convincing tribes to cede their land to the United States and divide remaining land into individual allotments. The commission also required Indians to claim membership in only one tribe and register on the Dawes Rolls**, what the government meant to be a definitive record of individuals with Indian blood.

We can see that it stopped quite short of it's intentions to be a definitive record. It became a mockery of the indigenous people it was supposed to record. The purpose for the Dawes Rolls is a mockery as well. **Their main goal was to remove the aboriginal indigenous people from their land, and accept land elsewhere they were not connected to**. Once again, how arrogant and haughty.

The **Curtis Act**, passed in 1898, targeted the Five Civilized Tribes (Cherokee, Choctaw, Chickasaw, Creek and Seminole), forcing them to accept allotments and register on the Dawes Rolls. The two acts—which came during a "**period of murky social context**" after the Civil War when white and black men were intermarrying with Native American women, **aimed to help the government keep track of "real" Indians while accelerating efforts to assimilate Indian people into white culture**, Smithers said.
https://newsmaven.io/indiancountrytoday/archive/paying-to-play-indian-the-dawes-rolls-and-the-legacy-of-5-indians-3yha0LldYUaH7smRsrks8A

If they were '*helping*' the government keep track of '*real*' Indians, **who were the fake Indians**? Or, the people they refused to acknowledge as the '*real*' indigenous people. They were put under the same pressures as today to get everyone to conform to the traditional European standard. It became **very**

hard for them to be themselves. Their land, way of life, (customs) and minds were being seized. They had to learn English as well.

The **Curtis Act** of 1898 was an amendment to the United States Dawes **Act**; it resulted in the **break-up of tribal governments and communal lands in Indian Territory** (now Oklahoma) of the Five Civilized Tribes of Indian Territory: the Choctaw, Chickasaw, Muscogee (Creek), Cherokee, and Seminole. Wikipedia

"By 1865, African Americans and white Americans were moving into the Midwest, into the Indian and Oklahoma territories, all vying for some patch of land they could call their own and live out their Jeffersonian view of independence," he said. "The federal government poured a lot of effort and energy into the Dawes Commission, but at the same time **it was very hard for both Native and American governments to keep track of who was who**."

The Dawes Commission set up tents in Indian Territory, said Bill Welge, director emeritus of the Oklahoma Historical Society's Office of American Indian Culture and Preservation. There, field clerks scoured written records, took oral testimony and generated enrollment cards **for individuals determined to have Indian blood**.

That included authentic Indians, Welge said. **But it also included lots of people with questionable heritage**.

"**Commissioners took advantage of their positions and enrolled people who had very minimal or questionable connections to the tribes**," he said. "**They were not adverse to taking money under the table**."

The implications of such shady practices are enormous now, Smithers said. Five-dollar Indians passed their

unearned benefits to heirs who still lay claim to tribal citizenship and associated privileges.

"**Now we have people who are white but who can trace their names back to the rolls used by tribal nations to ascertain who has rights as citizens**," he said. "**That means we have white people who have the ability to vote at large; it means political rights; it means the potential to influence tribal policy on a whole range of issues; it means people have access to health care, education and employment. The implications are quite profound for people who got away with fraud**."
https://newsmaven.io/indiancountrytoday/archive/paying-to-play-indian-the-dawes-rolls-and-the-legacy-of-5-indians-3yha0LldYUaH7smRsrks8A/

The actual Indians, or rather known as the **American Aborigines**, have since blamed the government for the mismanagement of a trust in their names, for well over 120 years, and now **the US Goverment owes them tens of billions of dollars**.

The dispute dates back to 1887, when Congress made the Interior Department the trustee for approximately 145 million acres of Indian lands in America.

Black Indians, or rather **Aborigines of America**, were supposed to benefit but **the government gave the majority of the land, legal tenders, tax reliefs and other federal specialized benefits to white settlers**; **who paid-off the citizenship administrative organizations, in order to become members of what is known as the Five Civilized Tribes in Indian Territory by Congress**.

White settlers sought to reap the benefits of the Aborigines. In fact, one example of that would be the complexity of how successful, but so openly fraudulent they did it.

In 1895, the white settlers were informed of what benefits the Indians were entitled to, so they traveled to the Dawes Roll Commission to inquire about having their names enlisted on the roll cards for full blooded and/or Freedman Indians of America lands.

In 1898, **the Dawes Roll acted as a census responsible for documenting records of one's ethnic backgrounds, in order to determine one's association with specific American Indian tribes**.

Also, it played an important role with determining which Indian tribes would get land allotments and other benefits that I detailed earlier, in return for abolishing their tribal governments and recognizing Federal laws. In order to receive the land, individual tribal members first had to apply, and then be deemed eligible by the Commission.

During the early part of the year 1902, **the US Government reacted with malicious intent, in developing a separate Freedmens list specifically designed to rule out all 'copper colored' Indians from receiving these newly established benefits by way of the Federal Government**.

What is also important to note, **the US Government listed all full blooded Indigenous Aborigines of America, mainly all of the Indians who they thought had African like features, as "Colored"** as their classification of race documented inside of the 1900
Census. https://imjustheretomakeyouthink.com/2017/04/03/untold-history-about-the-five-dollar-indians-culture-vultures-that-inherited-billions-of-dollars-million-acres-of-indian-land/

It is important to state that the racial classification for 'Black Indians' (Aboriginal Americans) began to change every ten years in conjunction with the national census. **Note, the indigenous people never called themselves Indians**. That label was applied to them by foreigners.

When the census began in 1790, the racial categories for the household population were "free white" persons, other "**free persons**" by color, and "**slaves**." Census-takers did not use standard forms in the early censuses.

For 1850-1880, the codes for enumerators were generally white (W), black (B) and **mulatto** (M). Beginning in 1850, the data item was labeled "**color**." In 1870, Chinese (C) and **Indian** (I) were added. In 1880, the data item was not labeled; it was "whether this person is..." In 1890, "Japanese," "**quadroon**" and "**octoroon**" were added.

Quadroon – a person who is a quarter black by descent. Wikipedia

Octoroon – a person who is one eighth black by descent. Wikipedia

In 1900, there were no specified categories on the census listing form, but the instructions called for enumerators to list "W" for white, "B" for "**black (or negro or negro descent)**", "Ch" for Chinese, "Jp" for Japanese, or "In" for Indian "as the case may be." **There was no mention of "quadroon" or "octoroon." This appears to be the first appearance of "negro"** (lower case) in the instructions but it was not listed on the form itself.

In 1910, the data item was called "**color or race**" **for the first time**. The instructions allowed for "Mu" for mulatto and "Ot" for other with an instruction to write in the race; "B" was called "**black**" only. The definition for "B" and "Mu" is: "For census purposes, **the term "black" (B) includes all persons who are evidently full blooded negroes**, while the term "mulatto" (Mu) includes all other persons having some proportion or perceptible trace of negro blood."

In 1920, there were no changes. In 1930, **there were specific instructions that used the term "Negro**." Persons who were mixed "White and Negro blood" were to be counted as "Negro" (apparently capitalized) no matter how small the share of "Negro blood." (This so-called "one-drop rule" or variations of it appeared in census instructions beginning in 1870.) Persons who were mixed white-Indian were to be counted as Indian "except where the percentage of Indian blood was very small or where he or she was regarded as White in the community." Any person who was "white" and "colored" was to be counted according to the "colored" race, and mixed colored races were to be counted according to the race of the father. There was an attempt in this census only to obtain figures for "Mex" (Mexicans), who were defined as "all persons born in Mexico, or having parents born in Mexico, who were not definitely White, Negro, Indian, Chinese, or Japanese."

In 1940, the only change was the elimination of the "Mex" category, and Mexicans "were to be listed as White unless they were definitely Indian or some race other than White."

In 1950, the census form listed the following categories: "White (W), Negro (Neg), American Indian (Ind), Japanese (Jap), Chinese (Chi), Filipino (Fil)," and other races to be spelled out. Note that the form did not contain the term "Black."

Beginning in 1960, the Census Bureau began to use forms similar to the ones in use today, with a single form for an entire household rather than having multiple households included on the form completed by an enumerator. Census forms were mailed to most people, but census-takers picked them up. The data item is called "Color or race" with categories for "White, Negro, American

Indian, Japanese, Chinese, Filipino, Hawaiian, Part Hawaiian, Aleut, Eskimo, (etc.)" Note that "**black**" **did not appear on the form**. The instructions called for census-takers to complete the race item by observation, and directed that Puerto Ricans, Mexicans, or other persons of Latin descent would be classified as "White" unless they were definitely "Negro," "Indian," or some other race. Southern European and Near Eastern nationalities also were to be considered "White." Asian Indians were to be classified as "Other," and "Hindu" was to be written in.

Self-identification was fully in place for 1970 and later censuses. The 1970 data item was still called "color or race" with the following response categories: "White, Negro or Black, Indian (Amer.), Japanese, Chinese, Filipino, Hawaiian, Korean, Other (with write-in)." **This was the first appearance of "black" since 1920**.

In 1980, the "race" item was not labeled; it read "Is this person…" The list of categories was expanded to include: "Vietnamese, Asian Indian, Guamanian, Samoan, Eskimo, Aleut." In addition, **the order of terms was changed to "Black or Negro**."

In 1990, the data item was relabeled; it was called "Race" for the first time, not "Color or Race." The categories remained the same as in 1980, but the "Asian or Pacific islander" categories were grouped together with a heading and an "Other API" category with a write-in was added.

In 2000, respondents were allowed to pick more than one race for the first time. The "race" data item retained essentially the same categories as in 1990 with a few adjustments. "**Black or Negro" became "Black, African Am., or Negro" marking the first appearance of "African-American" on the Census form**. The three Native American categories were grouped together as "American Indian or Alaska Native" with a write-in of tribe.

“Guamanian” became “Guamanian or Chamorro” and “Hawaiian” became “Native Hawaiian”. The “Other API” group was split into “Other Asian” and “Other Pacific Islander” with a separate write-in. Finally, “Other” became “Some other race” with its own write-in line. http://www.pewsocialtrends.org/2010/01/21/race-and-the-census-the-%E2%80%9Cnegro%E2%80%9D-controversy/

Paper Genocide: Since the beginnings of the African slave trade in America many Native persons unfortunately, **to the detriment of Native Heritage, were being listed as Black, Mulatto, Negro or just lumped together as “Colored” which did not allow for a distinction between us and Africans on paper**.

Walter Plecker of Virginia’s Vital Records began a paper genocide trend **that quickly spread thru out the 50 states and continues to this day.**

“Plecker was a member of the **Eugenics movement**, and Plecker had an agenda targeted at “**Indians**”, mixed race individuals and Blacks in the State of Virginia. **Plecker intentionally attempted to eliminate any evidence of any “Indians” in the State of Virginia, in order to purify the “white race”. Plecker modified birth records** in the State of Virginia, I learned that in some cases **Plecker actually ordered any documentation record on any individual that indicated “Indian” destroyed**, as well, **Plecker threatened midwives that indicated “Indian” as the race on the birth certificate**.

“Walter Ashby Plecker was the first registrar of Virginia’s Bureau of Vital Statistics, which records births, marriages and deaths. He accepted the job in 1912. For the next 34 years, **he led the effort to purify the white race in Virginia by forcing “Indians” and other nonwhites to classify themselves as blacks.** ***It amounted to bureaucratic genocide.”***

"**With the stroke of a pen, Plecker could write an individual into "Negro" status–and legal and social oblivion**. Plecker was only too willing to exercise that power, thus making him a figure of dread to Indians in general, but particularly to the Powhatan remnants in Rockbridge and Amherst counties, until his retirement and subsequent death in 1946."

"Plecker's no-nonsense approach made him a celebrity within the eugenics movement, which was increasingly losing support among scientists and becoming a platform for white supremacy. He spoke around the country, was widely published and wrote to every governor in the nation to urge passage of racial laws just as tough as Virginia's. He dined at the New York home of Harry H. Laughlin, the nation's leading eugenics advocate and an unabashed Nazi sympathizer."

"In 1932, Plecker gave a keynote speech at the Third International Conference on Eugenics in New York. Among those in attendance was Ernst Rudin of Germany who, 11 months later, would help write Hitler's eugenics law."

"In 1935, Plecker wrote to Walter Gross, the director of Germany's Bureau of Human Betterment and Eugenics. He outlined Virginia's racial purity laws and asked to be put on a mailing list for bulletins from Gross' department. **Plecker complimented the Third Reich for sterilizing 600 children in Algeria who were born to German women and black men.** "I hope this work is complete and not one has been missed," he wrote. "I sometimes regret that we have not the authority to put some measures in practice in Virginia."

"**Plecker changed and/or destroyed labels on vital records to classify Indians as "colored, mongrel, mulatto**," investigated the pedigrees of racially "suspect" citizens, and provided information to block or annul interracial marriages with Whites. He not only did this to Indians, but other races as well."

"Knowledge of this historical development is vitally necessary for those who are searching their Native heritage to understand why records in the Virginia Bureau of Vital Statistics are incorrect or missing." https://iloveancestry.com/paper-genocide-walter-plecker-eugenics-movement/

Paper Genocide is the deliberate and systematic destruction of Native American Indian culture, language, and identity as a unique racial group by way of the illegal and oppressive race reclassification imposed on Native American Indians or "Blood Indians" to the Non-Indian races of Black/African American. Google.com

Eugenics - the science of improving a human population by controlled breeding to increase the occurrence of desirable heritable characteristics. Developed largely by Francis Galton as a method of improving the human race, it fell into disfavor only after the perversion of its doctrines by the Nazis. Google.com

Simultaneously, **white U.S. citizens were allowed to become identified as Indians by paying the Dawes Commission a whopping total of just five dollars for each white adult and child to be listed on the Dawes Roll**.

On April 1st, 1902, public notices were passed around, detailing that other "claimants" can legally make their cases for Freedman Enrollment.

Singlehandedly allowing all white citizens the rights to legally steal the Indian lands of America (again), reparations, and optimized benefits set fourth by Federal law. Ironically, this was officially announced on the day most people would tell their very best April Fool's jokes.
https://imjustheretomakeyouthink.com/2017/04/03/untold-history-about-the-five-dollar-indians-culture-vultures-that-inherited-billions-of-dollars-million-acres-of-indian-land/

Historically, **immigrants** (**Europeans**) **were given special rights to take Native land**. According to our own legal tradition, Americans claim sovereignty over the territory of the US as **immigrants**, **precisely because the territories in question were someone else's homeland**: the Native Americans'.(American Aboriginal)

Since our country exists, we don't ask ourselves how or why. The legal foundation of the federal claim to dominion over territory is something called the **Doctrine of Discovery**, a notion that goes back five centuries. As European explorers sought new maritime passages and found new lands, popes granted European powers the authority to "**invade**, **search out**, **capture**, **vanquish and subdue**" the people they found.

Portugal, Spain, France and England claimed territory by planting a flag, a symbolic action known as "discovery". It made no difference whether the land in question was inhabited or not, since only Christians had conferred upon themselves the right to "discover" in this sense. By the logic of the papal bulls, and that of later charters to English explorers made by the English king or queen**, indigenous peoples had no rights to land or to legal recognition of any kind**. **Only immigrants did**.

The young American republic preserved this European doctrine. The US Supreme Court formalized the Doctrine of Discovery in three famous cases of 1823, 1831 and 1832. Chief Justice John

Marshall took for granted the obvious fact that America was the homeland of the Native Americans, "the rightful occupants of the soil". By the logic of "discovery", Native Americans had no rights because America was their homeland: "**Their power to dispose of the soil at their own will to whomsoever they pleased was denied by the original fundamental principle that discovery gave exclusive title to those who made it**."

In American law, **to have a homeland established no sovereignty over territory; only immigration created such authority**. According to Marshall, English charters and claims had established an "absolute and complete" title to the land of North America, which then "passed to the United States" in 1776. **The judicial magic of creating sovereignty and property is performed on behalf of immigrants and only on behalf of immigrants.**

From the perspective of modern human rights, or even of simple logic, there is much to criticize in the Doctrine of Discovery and in these rulings. In light of the first amendment of the constitution, separating church and state, papal bulls seem untenable as a source of American jurisprudence. When Marshall writes that "**conquest gives a title that the courts of the conqueror cannot deny**", it is easy to wonder whether anything more is being claimed in his rulings than that might makes right. Native American scholars have made all of these points, and aboriginal activists here and around the world have asked the pope to repeal the original bulls.

However flawed it may be, the Doctrine of Discovery is the law of the land, affirmed regularly by our highest court. In the 21st century, in New York v Oneida Indian Nation of New York, the supreme court cited Marshall's rulings and relied upon the Doctrine of Discovery as the basis of the federal government's dominion over land once controlled by Native Americans and

relied upon the Doctrine of Discovery as the basis of the federal government's dominion over land once controlled by Native Americans – which is to say, the entirety of the United States of America.
https://www.theguardian.com/commentisfree/2018/apr/28/us-government-native-americans-timothy-snyder

The **Indian Removal Act** was signed into law on May 28, 1830 by President Andrew Jackson. The law authorized the president to negotiate with southern Native American tribes for **their removal to federal territory west of the Mississippi River in exchange for white settlement of their ancestral lands**. The act has been referred to as a **unitary act of systematic genocide**, **because it completely discriminated against an ethnic group, to the point of certain death of vast numbers of its population**. The Act was signed by Jackson and it was strongly enforced under his administration and that of Martin Van Buren, which extended until 1841.

The Act was strongly supported by southern and northeast populations, with much resistance, however from native tribes and the Whig Party. The Cherokee worked together to stop this relocation, but were unsuccessful; they were eventually forcibly removed by the United States government in a march to the west that later became known as the **Trail of Tears**.

In the early 1800s**, the United States government began a systematic effort to remove American Indian tribes from the southeast.** The Chickasaw, Choctaw, Muscogee-Creek, Seminole, and original Cherokee Nations had been established as **autonomous nations** in the southeastern United States.

This acculturation was originally proposed by **George Washington** and was well under way among the Cherokee and Choctaw by the turn of the 19th century. In an effort to assimilate with American culture, Indians were encouraged to "**convert to**

Christianity; **learn to speak and read English**; and **adopt European-style economic practices such as the individual ownership of land and other property** (including, in some instances, the ownership of **African** slaves)." Thomas Jefferson's policy echoed Washington's proposition: **respect the Indians' rights to their homelands, and allow the Five Tribes to remain east of the Mississippi provided that they adopt behavior and cultural practices that are compatible with those of other Americans**. Jefferson encouraged practicing an agriculture-based society. Andrew Jackson sought to renew a policy of political and military action for the removal of the Indians from these lands and worked toward enacting a law for Indian removal. In his 1829 State of the Union address, Jackson called for removal.

The Indian Removal Act was put in place to give to the southern states the land that Indians had settled on. The act was passed in 1830, although dialogue had been ongoing since 1802 between Georgia and the federal government concerning such an event. Ethan Davis states that "**the federal government had promised Georgia that it would extinguish Indian title within the state's borders by purchase 'as soon as such purchase could be made upon reasonable terms**'". **As time passed, southern states began to speed up the process by posing the argument that the deal between Georgia and the federal government had no contract and that southern states could pass the law themselves. This scheme forced the national government to pass the Indian Removal Act** on May 28, 1830, in which President Jackson agreed to divide the United States territory west of the Mississippi into districts for tribes to replace the land from which they were removed.
https://www.theguardian.com/commentisfree/2018/apr/28/us-government-native-americans-timothy-snyder

Indian Removal Act, (May 28, 1830), **first major legislative departure from the U.S. policy of officially respecting the legal and political rights of the American Indians**. The act authorized the president to grant Indian tribes unsettled western prairie land in exchange for their desirable territories within state borders (especially in the Southeast), from which the tribes would be removed. **The rapid settlement of land east of the Mississippi River made it clear by the mid-1820s that the white man would not tolerate the presence of even peaceful Indians there**. https://www.britannica.com/topic/Indian-Removal-Act

The **Trail of Tears** was a series of forced relocations of Native Americans in the United States from their ancestral homelands in the Southeastern United States, to areas to the west (usually west of the Mississippi River) that had been designated as Indian Territory. The forced relocations were carried out by government authorities following the passage of the Indian Removal Act in 1830. **The relocated peoples suffered from exposure**, **disease**, **and starvation while en route to their new designated reserve**, **and many died before reaching their destinations**. The forced removals included members of the Cherokee, Muscogee (Creek), Seminole, Chickasaw, Choctaw, and Ponca nations. The phrase "Trail of Tears" originates from a description of the removal of many Native American tribes, including the infamous Cherokee Nation relocation in 1838.

Between 1830 and 1850, the Chickasaw, Choctaw, Creek, Seminole, and Cherokee people (including mixed-race and black slaves who lived among them) were forcibly removed from their traditional lands in the Southeastern United States, and relocated farther west. Those Native Americans who were relocated were forced to march to their destinations by state and local militias. The Cherokee removal in 1838 (the last forced removal east of the Mississippi) was brought on by the discovery of gold near

Dahlonega, Georgia in 1828, resulting in the Georgia Gold Rush. Approximately 2,000–8,000 of the 16,543 relocated Cherokee perished along the way.

In 1830, a group of Indians collectively referred to as the Five Civilized Tribes (the Cherokee, Chickasaw, Choctaw, Muscogee, and Seminole tribes) were living as autonomous nations in what would be later called the American Deep South. The process of cultural transformation, as proposed by George Washington and Henry Knox, was gaining momentum, especially among the Cherokee and Choctaw.

American settlers had been pressuring the federal government to remove Indians from the Southeast; **many settlers were encroaching on Indian lands**, **while others wanted more land made available to European ('Caucasian'/'white') settlers**. Although the effort was vehemently opposed by some, including U.S. Congressman Davy Crockett of Tennessee, President Andrew Jackson was able to gain Congressional passage of the Indian Removal Act of 1830, **which authorized the government to extinguish Indian title to lands in the Southeast**.

In 1831, the Choctaw became the first Nation to be removed, and their removal served as the model for all future relocations. After two wars, many Seminoles were removed in 1832. The Creek removal followed in 1834, the Chickasaw in 1837, and lastly the Cherokee in 1838. Some managed to evade the removals, however, and remained in their ancestral homelands; some Choctaw are living in Mississippi, Creek in Alabama and Florida, Cherokee in North Carolina, and Seminole in Florida. A small group of Seminole, fewer than 500, evaded forced removal; the modern Seminole Tribe of Florida is descended from these individuals. A small number of non-Native Americans who lived with the tribes, including some of African descent (some as slaves, and others as spouses or freedmen), also accompanied the Indians on the trek westward. By 1837, 46,000 Indians from the southeastern states had been removed from their homelands, thereby opening 25 million acres (100,000 km^2) for predominantly European settlement.

Prior to 1838, the fixed boundaries of these **autonomous tribal nations**, comprising large areas of the United States, **were subject to continual cession and annexation**, **in part due to pressure from squatters and the threat of military force in the newly declared U.S. territories**—federally administered regions whose boundaries supervened upon the Native treaty claims. As these territories became U.S. states, **state governments sought to dissolve the boundaries of the Indian nations within their borders**, **which were independent of state jurisdiction**, and to expropriate the land therein. These pressures were exacerbated by U.S. population growth and the expansion of slavery in the South, with the rapid development of cotton cultivation in the uplands following the invention of the cotton gin. Wikipedia

The roots of forced relocation lay in greed. The British Proclamation of 1763 designated the region between the Appalachian Mountains and the Mississippi River as Indian Territory. Although that region was to be protected for the exclusive use of indigenous peoples, large numbers of Euro-American land speculators and settlers soon entered. For the most part, the British and, later, U.S. governments ignored these acts of trespass.

In 1829 a gold rush occurred on Cherokee land in Georgia. Vast amounts of wealth were at stake: at their peak, Georgia mines produced approximately 300 ounces of gold a day. Land speculators soon demanded that the U.S. Congress devolve to the states the control of all real property owned by tribes and their members. That position was supported by Pres. Andrew Jackson, who was himself an avid speculator. Congress complied by passing the Indian Removal Act (1830). The act entitled the president to negotiate with the eastern nations to effect their removal to tracts of land west of the Mississippi and provided some $500,000 for transportation and for compensation to native landowners. Jackson reiterated his support for the act in various messages to Congress, notably "On Indian Removal" (1830) and "A Permanent Habitation for the American Indians" (1835), which illuminated his political justifications for removal and described some of the outcomes he expected would derive from the relocation process.

Indigenous reactions to the Indian Removal Act varied. The Southeast Indians were for the most part tightly organized and heavily invested in agriculture. **The farms of the most populous tribes—the Choctaw, Creek, Chickasaw, Seminole, and Cherokee—were particularly coveted by outsiders because they were located in prime agricultural areas and were very well developed**. **This meant that speculators who purchased such properties could immediately turn a profit: fields had already been cleared, pastures fenced, barns and houses built, and the like.** Thus, the Southeast tribes approached federal negotiations with the goal of either reimbursement for or protection of their members' investments.

The Choctaw were the first polity to finalize negotiations: in 1830 they agreed to cede their real property for western land, transportation for themselves and their goods, and logistical support during and after the journey. However, the federal government had no experience in transporting large numbers of civilians, let alone their household effects, farming equipment, and livestock. **Bureaucratic ineptitude and corruption caused many Choctaw to die from exposure**, **malnutrition**, **exhaustion**, **and disease while traveling**.

The Chickasaw signed an initial removal agreement as early as 1830, but negotiations were not finalized until 1832. Skeptical of federal assurances regarding reimbursement for their property, members of the Chickasaw nation sold their landholdings at a profit and financed their own transportation. As a result, their journey, which took place in 1837, had fewer problems than did those of the other Southeast tribes.

The Creek also finalized a removal agreement in 1832. However, Euro-American settlers and speculators moved into the planned Creek cessions prematurely, causing conflicts, delays, and fraudulent land sales that delayed the Creek journey until 1836. **Federal authorities once again proved incompetent and corrupt, and many Creek people died**, **often from the same preventable causes that had killed Choctaw** travelers. A small group of Seminole leaders negotiated a removal agreement in 1832, but a majority of the tribe protested that the signatories had no authority to represent them. The United States insisted that the agreement should hold, instigating such fierce resistance to removal that the ensuing conflict became known as the Second Seminole War (1835–42). Although many were eventually captured and removed to the west, a substantial number of Seminole people managed to elude the authorities and remain in Florida. https://www.britannica.com/event/Trail-of-Tears

Homestead Act of 1862 The Law: Federal legislation making public land available to settlers for free signed into law on May 20, 1862.

The Homestead Act accelerated settlement of western lands in the United States. Initiated in response to pressure for the disposition of public lands, the act transferred ownership of property to U.S. citizens or **immigrants** willing to establish residence on the land and to make improvements and cultivate crops. **A significant number of beneficiaries of the act were immigrants from Europe**.
http://immigrationtounitedstates.org/554-homestead-act-of-1862.html

Beginning in 1863, the words "free land" became a siren call for landless U.S. citizens, freed slaves and **hundreds of thousands of European immigrants** after President Abraham Lincoln signed the Homestead Act. The act, which offered 160 acres of land to any qualified homesteader who paid a modest filing fee, built a home, planted at least 10 acres of crops and remained on his or her claim for at least five years, has been called the most important act ever passed for the benefit of the American people. **It ultimately helped create the most productive agricultural economy the world has ever seen. The lure of *free* land prompted millions of Europeans to immigrate to the United States in the years following the Civil War**. Some left their homelands because of crop failures and economic depression. Others sought political and religious freedom, or to escape constant warfare. They came from **Germany** and **Czechoslovakia**, from **Sweden** and **Norway**, from **England** and **Russia**.

Between 1870 and 1900, **more than two million immigrants had settled on the Great Plains**. You can still find their descendants living in places like Denmark, Kansas; Bruno, Nebraska; New Holland, South Dakota; Bismarck, North Dakota; and Glasgow, Montana.

https://www.grit.com/farm-and-garden/homestead-act-of-1862

When the Europeans arrived, they might have thought the land was uninhabited because the local Natives were smart enough not to show their faces right away. But when they found out that there were already people here, why did they just barge in, anyway? It was because they thought they were actually **superior beings**. **When we take an honest look at the Natives as they lived at the time, we see that they had highly developed civilizations, with complex languages and social organizations, highly developed spirituality, and advanced knowledge of natural medicines, farming and hunting. They**

kept the land in pristine condition. In no way were they inferior to the Europeans. Unfortunately, the Europeans had **closed minds** and **superior weapons**, plus they had diseases that did much of the work of "ethnic cleansing" for them. Whole populations were wiped out by smallpox and other diseases.

Native Americans had **three choices**, all forced on them at one time or another**. They could assimilate with the encroaching European population** – which didn't work very well. More on that below. **Or they could be relocated**. More on that below, as well. The third option was **genocide** – and when you consider that the original population of Natives in the area now known as the United States was about 15 million, and that at its lowest, the population of Native Americans was only about 250,000 in 1900, you have to admit that **most of the Natives were killed by genocide**. Either they died of diseases such as smallpox and cholera, were massacred in wars, or they died of starvation, alcoholism or illness endemic to the harsh life on the reservations. Many died in the forced relocations mandated by the Homestead Acts.

Why did the Natives enter into all those land treaties that essentially gave their land to the Europeans, anyway? Well, you have to understand, first of all, that the Native cultures in North America **did not have the concept of private ownership of land**. **Land was something to be shared by all**. **Land was to be protected and given respect**, and **humans were seen as having a symbiotic relationship with the land**. The land provided sustenance to the people, who took care of the land.

Richard Greener wrote, "It was common for one tribe to grant permission to another to hunt and fish nearby themselves on a regular basis. Fences, real and imagined, were not a part of their culture. Naturally, it was polite to ask before setting up operations too close to where others lived, but refusal in matters of this sort was considered rude. As a sign of gratitude, small trinkets were usually offered by the tribe seeking temporary admission and cheerfully accepted by those already there. It was clearly understood to be a sort of short-term rental arrangement." It's easy to see, when you look at history this way, why the Natives were so angry when they found out that they were no longer welcome in the lands settled by the Europeans. Still, **the Natives are**, **as a whole**, **honorable people**, and they believed the Europeans when they were promised lands further west. Their descendants are still wondering why the United States government could not manage to honor and keep the original treaties.

There was a separate Homestead act for Native Americans (the Indian Homestead Act, or Dawes Act), but it failed because the allotments for Natives were always chosen by the government, **and they were generally of inferior quality**, **making it hard for Native to farm the land**. Frustrated, many homesteaders sold their land to white settlers. Secondly, **those to whom land was granted had to choose a European name**. **The act ended up fragmenting tribes and accelerating cultural erosion**.

https://mettahu.wordpress.com/2013/11/14/the-effect-of-the-homestead-act-on-native-americans/

Manifest Destiny: The religious belief that the United States should expand from the Atlantic Ocean to the Pacific Ocean in the name of God.
http://www.californiaindianeducation.org/student_works/manifest_destiny_crimes/

In the 19th century, **manifest destiny** was a widely held belief in the United States that its settlers were destined to expand across North America. There are three basic themes to manifest destiny:

- The special virtues of the American people and their institutions
- The mission of the United States to redeem and remake the west in the image of agrarian America
- An irresistible destiny to accomplish this essential duty. Wikipedia

Expansion westward seemed perfectly natural to many Americans in the mid-nineteenth century. Like the Massachusetts Puritans who hoped to build a "city upon a hill, "courageous pioneers believed that America had a **divine obligation to stretch the boundaries of their noble republic to the Pacific Ocean**. Independence had been won in the Revolution and reaffirmed in the War of 1812. The spirit of nationalism that swept the nation in the next two decades demanded more territory. The "every man is equal" mentality of the Jacksonian Era fueled this optimism. Now, with territory up to the Mississippi River claimed and settled and the Louisiana Purchase explored, Americans headed west in droves. Newspaper editor JOHN O'SULLIVAN coined the term "**MANIFEST DESTINY**" in 1845 to describe the essence of this mindset.

The religious fervor spawned by the Second Great Awakening created another incentive for the drive west. Indeed, **many settlers believed that God himself blessed the growth of the American nation**. The **Native Americans were considered heathens**. **By Christianizing the tribes**, American missionaries believed they could save souls and they became among the first to cross the Mississippi River.

Economic motives were paramount for others. The fur trade had been dominated by European trading companies since colonial times. German immigrant John Jacob Astor was one of the first American entrepreneurs to challenge the Europeans. He became a millionaire in the process. The desire for more land brought aspiring homesteaders to the frontier. When gold was discovered in California in 1848, the number of migrants increased even more.

At the heart of manifest destiny was the pervasive belief in American cultural and racial superiority. Native Americans had long been perceived as inferior, and efforts to "**civilize**" them had been widespread since the days of John Smith and MILES STANDISH. The Hispanics who ruled Texas and the lucrative ports of California were also seen as "backward." http://www.ushistory.org/us/29.asp

Westward expansion and manifest destiny had a very negative effect on the Mexicans and on the Native Americans. As Americans wanted to expand westward, **they continued to view the Native Americans as being in the way and holding back the progress of our country**. In the 1830s, the Native Americans were forcibly removed from their lands east of the Mississippi River to lands west of the Mississippi River. Many Native Americans died as a result of the forced relocation, which often is referred to as the Trail of Tears. As Americans began to expand beyond the Mississippi River, **Americans again viewed the Native Americans as holding back the progress of our country**. New policies were developed placing Native Americans on reservations. **These policies disrupted and**, **in some cases**, **destroyed their way of life.** These policies were made with the interests of the Americans in mind, not with the interests of the Native Americans in mind. Westward expansion and manifest destiny were not positive events for the Native Americans. https://www.enotes.com/homework-help/what-impact-did-manifest-destiny-westward-377364

The self-serving concept of manifest destiny, the belief that the expansion of the United States was divinely ordained, justifiable, and inevitable, was used to rationalize the

removal of American Indians from their native homelands. In the minds of white Americans, the Indians were not using the land to its full potential as they reserved large tracts of unspoiled land for hunting, leaving the land uncultivated. If it was not being cultivated, then the land was being wasted. Americans declared that it was their duty, their manifest destiny, which compelled them to seize, settle, and cultivate the land. Not surprisingly, the most active supporters of manifest destiny and proponents of Indian removal were those who practiced **land speculation**. Land speculators bought large tracts of land with the expectation that the land would quickly increase in value as more people settled in the west and demand for that western land increased. As the western land was admitted into the Union, it would consequently increase in value. https://americanexperience.si.edu/wp-content/uploads/2015/02/Manifest-Destiny-and-Indian-Removal.pdf

In Conclusion

The Doctrine of Discovery has been a disaster to the Aboriginal Americans. (so-called Blacks, Negroes, Colored or African American) The amount of loss and tragedy inflicted upon the indigenous people, environment, land, plants, and animals cannot be calculated. The most important factor of it is the doctrine is a pattern or system of thought. It can be boiled down to a system of ideas. It lays out the blueprints for dehumanization and destruction. When the pope instructs the explorers (exploiters) to **invade**, it doesn't just consist of a physical takeover of land. It also involves and invasion of the mind, emotions, and spirit as well. As discussed earlier, Aboriginal Americans (copper colored) were made to assimilate into European culture. They were made to speak English. They were made to dress and think like foreigners. How asinine is it for Europeans to set themselves as the standard for others to follow. These are all different aspects of invasion. **Capture** carries the same connotations. Synonyms for capture are to arrest, abduct, imprison, occupation, seize, take acquire, snatch, or trap. All of these things were, and are still being done to Aboriginal Americans. Synonyms for **vanquish** are, conquer, defeat (utterly), trounce, annihilate, crush, and subjugate. All these techniques are hidden behind Christianity. These acts directly contrast everything their master teacher (Jesus) told them. These were methods used to destroy an entire continent. These actions were just and lawful according the pope's who issued these directives. The word **subdue** means, to conquer and reduce to subjection," from Old French souduire, but this meant "deceive, seduce." Isn't Satan the deceiver? A legal way was devised to colonize and steal. https://www.etymonline.com/search?q=subdue

Perpetual means mid-14c., from Old French perpetuel "without end" (12c.) and directly from Latin perpetualis "universal," in Medieval Latin "permanent," from perpetuus "continuous, universal," from perpetis, genitive of Old Latin perpes "lasting," https://www.etymonline.com/word/perpetual The time frame for slavery could not be made any clearer. Synonyms for perpetual are infinite, constant, ceaseless, eternal, endless, permanent, and continued. This is the amount of time slavery is supposed to last.

This was a long term plan for 'enemies of Christ'. Justified because the indigenous people in those lands didn't share the same belief system. The courts further legitimized this beastly system by codifying it into law. Citing the same papal bulls issued by a foreign leader (pope) of an ecclesiastical body politic.

Synonyms for haughty are: cavalier, contemptuous, indifferent, snobbish, conceited, distant, egotistical, high-and-mighty, and detached. This was the attitude of the immigrants towards the Aboriginal Americans, which is shared by many of their descendants today when faced with issues in regards to the descendants of the Aboriginal Americans (Blacks, Negroes, Colored, African-American). There seems to be an air of the same superiority that the original immigrants brought with them passed down to their later generations until today. There is a general lack of feeling and understanding for concerns of the Aboriginal Americans today.

Convert means cause to **change in form**, **character**, or **function**, **change or be able to change from one form to another**, change (money, stocks, or units in which a quantity is expressed) (**or people**) into others of a different kind, adapt (a building) (**or a people**) to make it suitable for a new purpose. https://www.google.com/search?source=hp&ei=EWiQXImlMqPijwS4jpmoCw&q=etymology+of+convert&btnK=Google+Search&oq=etymology+of+convert&gs_l=psy-ab.3..0j0i22i30l2.807.17531..17773...2.0..0.352.2236.20j1j1j1....2..0....1..gws-wiz.....0..35i39j0i131j0i67j0i20i263j0i10j0i131i20i263._2gH11bJrZM

It was not simply a conversion of faith, it was a conversion into European American culture. It was a change of, as stated above, 'from one form to another'. From the natural Aboriginal American form to the European American model was the change. The people were the units; and had to adapt themselves to the new European American culture for a 'suitable new purpose'.

The land was also converted. It went from balance in a delicate ecology to an abused, misused, negatively affected, piece of equipment for personal ownership.

It can be seen that all the fancy talk disguised as God's will is a ruse. This all falls under fraud and the Aboriginal copper colored Americans are owed incalculable amounts of money for restitution.

All emphasis is mine.

www.ingramcontent.com/pod-product-compliance
Ingram Content Group UK Ltd.
Pitfield, Milton Keynes, MK11 3LW, UK
UKHW051135260726
13967UKWH00010B/3065

9 780359 616732